STREET JAZZ AND MODERN DANCE

RITA STOREY

SEA-TO-SEA
Mankato Collingwood London

LINCOLN ELEMENTARY SCHOOL

STREET JAZZ

AND MODERN DANCE

Street jazz dance began in the United States. In the 1920s, people went to dance halls to dance to a new type of music, called jazz. Jazz dancing was very popular in places where there were large black communities, such as New Orleans in the South, and Harlem in New York. Many dances were invented at this time, such as the black bottom, the lindy hop, the charleston, and the jitterbug.

Jazz dancing has gone through many changes since those early days. Today there is a form of jazz dancing called "street jazz." It includes breakdancing, hip hop, and modern tap dancing. But one thing remains the same—these dances are created in the clubs and on the streets by ordinary people who just love to dance.

Why should *I* dance?

Dancing is good for everyone. It's a great way to get in shape. All types of dancing are a form of aerobic exercise, which encourages your heart and lungs to work hard. Over time, this will help them to become stronger and get *you* in better shape.

The food we eat provides our body with the energy it needs to work properly. But if we eat more calories than our body needs, these are stored as fat. Dancing makes your body burn off calories. Your muscles will strengthen and become firmer, and your body will become more toned.

Dancing makes you happy

When you exercise, your brain makes a hormone called seratonin, which makes you feel happy. So if you're feeling miserable, put down the chocolate, put on the music, and get dancing.

There are so many types of dance there really is something for everyone. You can do the dance moves in this book on your own or with a friend, and work at a pace that suits you.

Dancing can even boost your brain power. Putting together dance steps increases your coordination and helps keep your mind alert.

Last but not least, dancing is fun. So what are you waiting for? Turn up the music and get moving!

Contents

Let's get moving

Why do I have to warm up?

Before you learn any new dance steps and begin to put them together, it is important to warm up your muscles so you don't get a cramp or strain a muscle. You may only be able to do the exercises a couple of times to start with, but don't give up. Just do a few more repeats each time. A warmup should last about ten minutes.

There are warmup moves in each of the four books in the *Get Dancing* series. You can combine them to make a routine.

Aerobic exercises

The first set of exercises is aerobic, which means it improves your breathing and circulation. Aerobic exercise increases your oxygen intake by making your heart beat faster. To do it, you have to keep on the move all the time. Each set of aerobic exercises is designed to be repeated. If you are not used to exercise and feel your pulse starting to race, stop and jog on the spot to keep warm.

AEROBIC EXERCISE
GRAPEVINE

1 Step to the left with the left foot.

2 Move right foot behind left foot.

3 Step onto the right foot.

4 Bring feet together.

Repeat the 4 steps to the left. Do the sequence 5 times to each side.

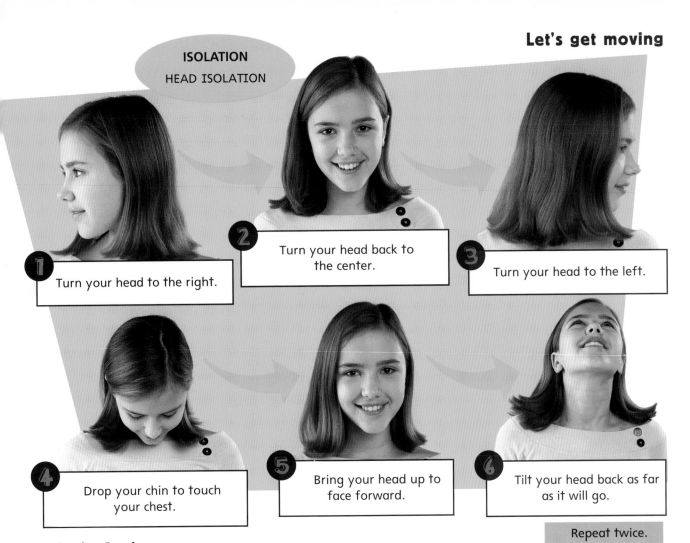

ISOLATION

HEAD ISOLATION

1 Turn your head to the right.

2 Turn your head back to the center.

3 Turn your head to the left.

4 Drop your chin to touch your chest.

5 Bring your head up to face forward.

6 Tilt your head back as far as it will go.

Repeat twice.

Body isolations

The second set of exercises is a body isolation. This type of exercise teaches you to move parts of your body individually, which is important for street jazz dancing.

What to wear

Wear something comfortable to do a warmup, such as loose-fitting leggings (not jeans), a T-shirt, and a loose, long-sleeved top you can take off when you have warmed up.

You can do the routine in bare feet, sneakers, or jazz shoes. Don't do it in socks, or you may slip.

Dance to the music

You will need at least two pieces of music for the warmup. The first is for the aerobic exercises. It should be energetic and upbeat, to make everyone feel enthusiastic. It can also be used for body isolations, which are sharp, quick moves.

The second piece of music will be used for the stretches and toning exercises (see page 6). Gentle, relaxing music is best for this part of the warmup.

Let's get moving

Stretches

The most important thing to remember about stretches is that they should be done gradually. It's easy to pull a muscle by pushing yourself too hard, too soon.

Try doing the exercises every day and stretching just a little bit further each time. If it hurts, STOP. You may feel a little stiff the next day if you haven't been exercising regularly, but you shouldn't be in pain. If you are, you have stretched too hard. Stop for a few days and then slowly start building the stretches up again.

Toning exercises

These exercises are to strengthen and tone particular muscles, giving you a better body shape and strong muscles to hold the dance moves.

STRETCH AND TONE 1
ARM STRETCH

Stand with your feet apart, toes facing the front, and hips square. Stretch up your right arm, then your left arm, as high as you can.

Repeat 5 times.

STRETCH AND TONE 2
LEG STRETCH

1 Stand with your feet apart, toes facing the front, and your knees bent. Put the palms of your hands flat on the floor.

2 Straighten your legs as much as you can without lifting your hands off the floor.

Repeat 5 times.

Cool it!

At the end of a dance session, it is important to do a cool-down routine to help prevent stiffness the next day. The routine concentrates on stretching exercises that stretch out and relax the muscles. To be effective, each stretch should be held for a slow count of ten. A cool-down routine should last for five to ten minutes.

Each of the four books in the *Get Dancing* series contains cool-down stretches. You can use the two shown here, or a combination from different books.

Hold each move for a slow count of 10.

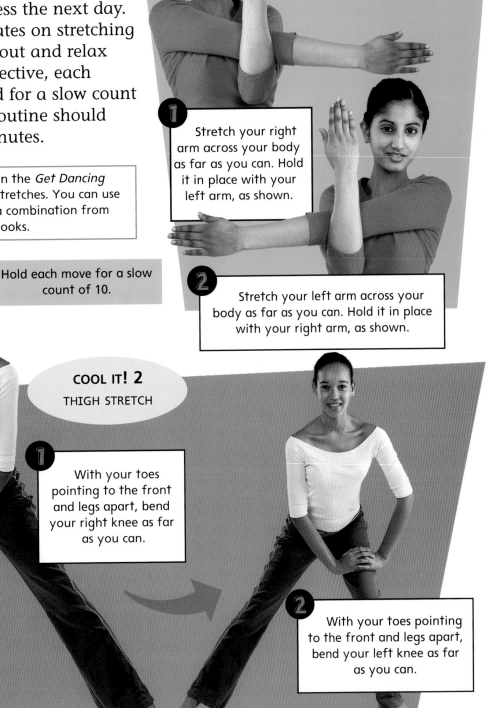

COOL IT! 1
UPPER ARM STRETCH

1 Stretch your right arm across your body as far as you can. Hold it in place with your left arm, as shown.

2 Stretch your left arm across your body as far as you can. Hold it in place with your right arm, as shown.

COOL IT! 2
THIGH STRETCH

1 With your toes pointing to the front and legs apart, bend your right knee as far as you can.

2 With your toes pointing to the front and legs apart, bend your left knee as far as you can.

Breakdancing

Breakdancing has some basic steps, although if you watch an expert breakdancer, these are not always obvious because dancers add moves to make their dances very individual.

The moves

There are two basic sets of moves in breakdancing: toprock and downrock. Other moves, such as power moves, locking, popping, moonwalking, uprock, and freezes, can be added to these (see pages 10–13).

Toprock

The first stage of breakdancing is toprock, or shuffling. This series of moves is designed to create a clear circle on the dancefloor before going on to downrock and other moves.

TOPROCK

1 Hop forward onto the ball of your right foot.

2 Hop back onto your left foot.

3 Put your right foot behind and to the left. Turn to the left.

4 Put your left foot back again.

5 Start again. This time, hop forward onto the ball of your left foot.

HOW BREAKDANCING STARTED

In the 1970s, a new style of street dancing emerged from Los Angeles and New York. It was based on fast footwork and acrobatic head and hand spins. At first, this type of dance was called "b-boying," but later it became known as breakdancing.

"Get on the Good Foot"
The origins of breakdancing can be traced back to a singer called James Brown. In the 1960s, he released a record called "Get on the Good Foot." When he sang the song on stage, he performed some very athletic dance moves, and these probably inspired some of the breakdancing moves. (One particular move, which became known as "The Good Foot," consisted of holding one knee high for a beat and then raising the other knee before the first foot hit the ground.)

Martial arts
Breakdancing was also influenced by the martial arts capoeira and kung fu, which people learned for self-defense.

A breakdancer shows off a power move to a crowd of onlookers.

Downrock

Downrock

The second stage of breakdancing is downrock—moves that take place low on the floor. The most basic downrock move is the six-step downrock shown below, which also forms the basis of more complex steps.

Power moves

The more difficult downrock moves are called power moves. The most common of these are the windmill, headspins, flares, and jackhammers. These moves require great skill and take months to learn.

Freezes

Each session of breakdancing ends with a freeze. The dancer freezes his body into a pose and remains motionless for a while.

DOWNROCK
(6 STEPS)

1 Crouch down on the floor as though you are about to do a push-up.

2 Without moving your left leg, move the knee of your right leg up toward your chest.

3 Without moving your right leg, move the knee of your left leg up toward your chest.

4 Move your right leg in an arc, moving your hands out of the way as your leg comes around.

5 Continue to swing your right leg.

FROM BREAKDANCING TO HIP HOP

Hip hop is a youth culture that began among Black American and Puerto Rican young people in the south Bronx. It was pioneered by a group of DJs who were influenced by DJs such as Grandmaster Flash and Afrika Bambaataa. Using vinyl records, turntables, and mixing techniques, they created a new, energetic dance scene that included breakdancing.

Breakdance battles

Sometimes rival street gangs held breakdance battles to settle scores, instead of fighting. Dancers (called "crews") competed by performing complicated breakdancing routines. The slickest dancers were the winners.

Movie stars

The crews inspired movies about dance battles, such as *Wild Style*, *Beat Street*, and *Flashdance*. Often, the actual crews starred in the movies, because it was almost impossible to train professional dancers to breakdance as well as the crews could. Individual crew members became movie stars.

Today, breakdancing has moved on into hip hop. This emphasizes footwork rather than the acrobatic moves of breakdancing. Together with rap music, DJ-ing, and graffiti art, hip hop is an important part of hip-hop culture.

6 Jump your left leg over your right leg. Begin again at step 1.

Locking and popping

Breakdancing routines can also include moves called locking, popping, and moonwalking.

Locking
Locking is a "move and then freeze" action. It was based on the way that robots in sci-fi movies moved. This way of dancing gives the dancer a mechanical look.

Popping
Popping is similar to locking, but is made up of a series of set poses linked by swift movements. It is also called "electric boogaloo."

Moonwalking
This step makes you appear to be traveling across the floor on a moving travelator.

LOCKING

POPPING

1 Locking starts with the limbs collapsing.

2 Then they are locked, or snapped, back into place.

1 In popping, the move from one pose to another is robotic, with exact stops and starts. The joints are "popped" one after the other.

THE MUSIC VIDEO

The first music videos to be produced were just movies of bands performing their music. Soon, however, the music video became a miniature movie that told a story, and used special effects. Music videos became a way of helping sell music, and were almost as important as the music itself.

Michael Jackson

In the 1980s and 1990s, the singer Michael Jackson was very successful. He was famous for his dancing, particularly moonwalking, which was an extension of locking and popping. In the videos "Billie Jean," "Beat It," and "Thriller," the dance element was as strong as the music.

Other artists included dance in their acts, too. Madonna, Janet Jackson, and boy bands like the Backstreet Boys and N.Sync swapped guitars and musical instruments for energetic dance routines to accompany their songs. Both music videos and live stage performances included big-production dance routines.

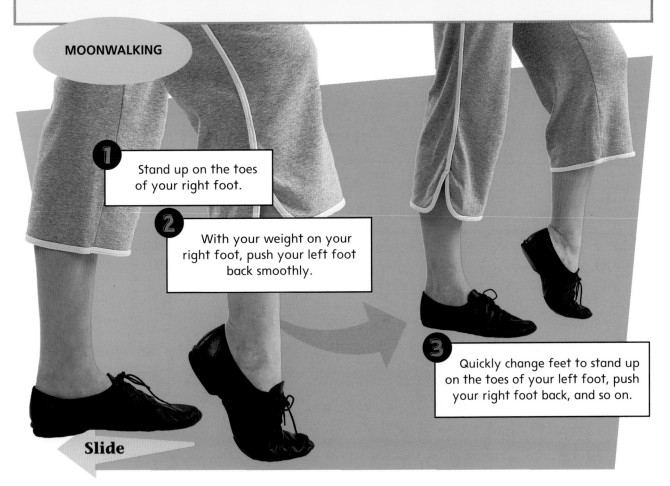

MOONWALKING

1 Stand up on the toes of your right foot.

2 With your weight on your right foot, push your left foot back smoothly.

3 Quickly change feet to stand up on the toes of your left foot, push your right foot back, and so on.

Slide

Hip-hop dancing

Hip-hop dancing has grown out of breakdancing. Its lively, exciting dance routines are great fun to perform in a group. Remember the dance battles between rival gangs? (See page 11.) Why don't you gather some friends together and stage your own friendly dance battle? Create at least two crews, choose crew names, select some music, start practicing, and then battle it out! Turn to page 20 for some ideas about how to stage the dance battle.

HIP-HOP MOVE **1**

1 Stand with your feet apart and your arms at shoulder height, with your elbows bent and hands in fists.

2 Step your left foot across your body to the right. Open your arms strongly out to the side, with a punching action.

3 Return to position 1. Repeat to the other side, stepping your right foot across your body to the left.

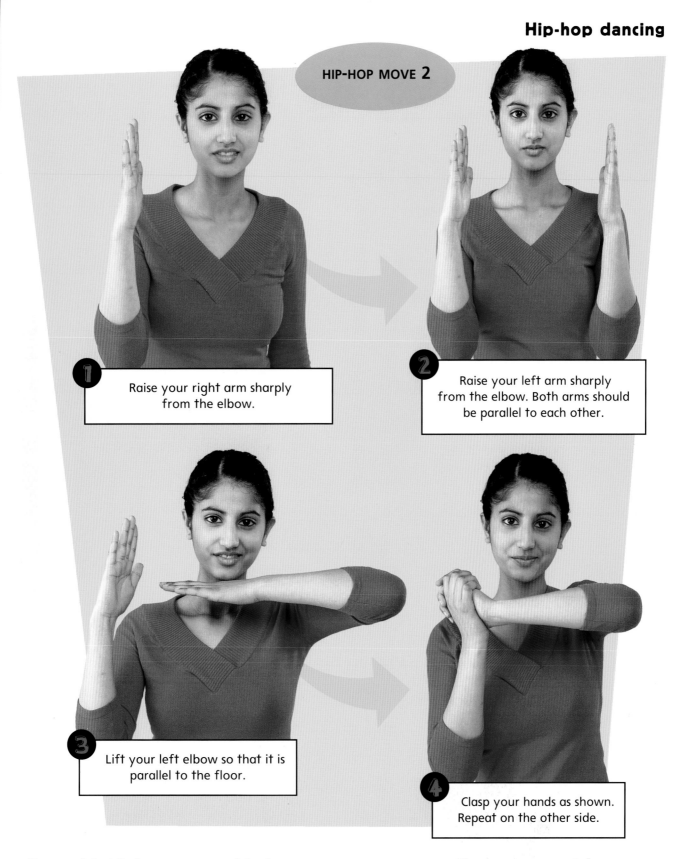

HIP-HOP MOVE 2

1 Raise your right arm sharply from the elbow.

2 Raise your left arm sharply from the elbow. Both arms should be parallel to each other.

3 Lift your left elbow so that it is parallel to the floor.

4 Clasp your hands as shown. Repeat on the other side.

Pages 14–19 demonstrate hip-hop dance steps that can be used in your dance battle, although there are many more that you can pick up from watching the dance routines of your favorite hip-hop artists.

Hip-hop dancing

HIP-HOP MOVE 3

1 With your feet wide apart, bend your knees and rest your hands by your knees, with your thumbs facing backward.

2 Keeping your left leg as still as you can, sharply turn your right leg and right shoulder in toward the middle.

3 Return to position 1.

4 Keeping your right leg as still as you can, turn your left leg and left shoulder in toward the middle. Then return to position 1.

Hip-hop dancing

1 Stand with your feet apart, your right hand held at shoulder height, and your right arm parallel to the ground.

HIP-HOP MOVE 5

2 Kick your right leg behind you, with the knee bent up at the back. Put your foot down (standing with your feet apart).

3 With both knees bent and hands clasped together, reach out to the left...

6 Kick your left leg behind you, with the knee bent up at the back. Return to position 1.

5 ...and then to the right.

4 ...and then in front...

Battle it out

You've practiced the moves and routines, and now you are ready to perform your dance battle. Remember that because of hip hop's links with martial arts (see page 9), the dance moves are nearly always sharp, strong, and very quick. The style of the dancing is very important. You need to dance with real confidence and lots of "attitude." This is your opportunity to show what you can do. Let battle commence!

What to wear

Hip-hop dancewear is very urban in style. It consists of sweats, leggings, T-shirts, baggy jeans, hoods, and lycra tops. These are often worn with pull-on hats.

Many of the expensive brand names use graffiti art or aerosol art in their designs. You could create a style for your crew by customizing T-shirts with your own graffiti logo.

Hip-hop dancing is very energetic, so remember to choose clothes that are comfortable and are not going to make you feel too hot.

You can design a logo on the computer and then print it on special paper that will transfer the logo to a T-shirt when an iron is applied to it.

Friendly rivalry is in the air as two crews prepare for their dance battle.

Stage it

Graffiti was part of early hip-hop culture. In the 1970s, New York subways were covered in the bubble writing of various gangs, who used spray paint to leave their signature or "tag," as it was called.

If you intend to perform your dance battle in front of an audience, you might like to use graffiti as a backdrop. You could paint your crew names in the bubble writing style.

Other possibilities would be to paint images of the New York subway or the back streets of Manhattan on a backdrop. Both of these would form a monochrome background, so dancers could provide a contrast by wearing really colorful clothing.

Dance to the music

At first, hip hop was closely linked with "gangsta" culture in inner cities. Many early tracks by artists such as Eminem had violent, angry lyrics. But now some of the music has moved away from these angry beginnings. Many artists on the pop music scene are including hip-hop rhythms in their songs and dancing hip-hop moves. For your friendly dance battle you may prefer music by artists such as the Black-eyed Peas, Justin Timberlake, or Britney Spears.

Tap dancing

Until fairly recently, tap dancing had a dated image. All that changed when the stage show *Stomp* exploded onto the scene. It was created by two British musicians. They used everyday objects, such as brooms and garbage can lids, to create noisy, energetic rhythms, accompanied by dancing.

Modern tap dance is full of possibilities. Create a dance that is based on making sounds and movements with an everyday object. Devise your own tap routine, interspersed with moves like those shown here. Turn to pages 26–27 to learn some tap steps.

Dance to the music

Try performing your own version of *Stomp*. Use everyday objects to make different percussion sounds. Wooden spoons, brooms, metal colanders, buckets, and garbage cans are perfect for creating your own dance rhythms.

CLEAN SWEEP
ROUTINE

1 Thump the end of the brush on the floor, striking it with the wooden part.

Clonk

Swishhhhh Swishhhhh

2 Push the brush vigorously back and forth across the floor.

3 Twirl the brush around in the air (but be aware of other people and your surroundings).

22

STOMP OUT LOUD

Stomp was created in 1991 by Luke Cresswell and Steve McNicholas, both musicians and performers. They describe the show as a unique combination of percussion, movement, and visual comedy.

Stomp goes to America

The DVD *Stomp Out Loud* is filmed in the back streets of Manhattan. Its dance routines are unconventional and based on the noises that are around us all the time. A basketball being thrown against a wall, knives chopping in a kitchen, and garbage can lids crashing are all used to create the "music" that accompanies the foot stomp of the dancing.

Tap Dogs

In 1995, an Australian called Dein Perry put together a dance troupe called *Tap Dogs* to dance tap, but not tap as we traditionally know it. Dancers perform in workboots rather than tap shoes, to a wide selection of music. The result is noisy, energetic, and "street."

The dancers in *Stomp* performing a routine using yard brooms.

Tap dancing

What to wear

This style of dance celebrates very ordinary everyday life. The clothes you wear to perform the dances can do the same. So mechanic's overalls, chef's pants, denim, aprons, or other simple work clothes can be selected to suit the objects that you are using.

GARBAGE CAN CRASH

1 Hook your foot under the handle of a garbage can lid and tap out a beat on the floor.

These photos show some ideas to include in a routine using a metal garbage can as your main prop. Invent some more steps for your "garbage can crash." You can have fun making plenty of noise!

2 Smash the lids on the floor.

3 Bang the lids together.

4 Use the garbage can as a drum.

Tap dancing

Here are some basic tap steps. They can be combined into the Tap Steps routine on page 27, or added to the Clean Sweep routine on page 22.

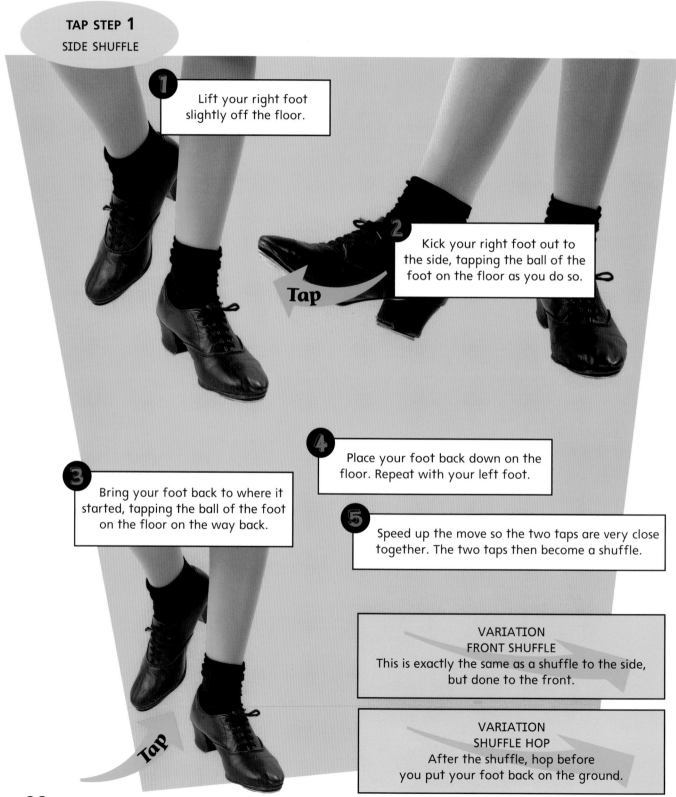

TAP STEP 1
SIDE SHUFFLE

1 Lift your right foot slightly off the floor.

2 Kick your right foot out to the side, tapping the ball of the foot on the floor as you do so.

Tap

3 Bring your foot back to where it started, tapping the ball of the foot on the floor on the way back.

4 Place your foot back down on the floor. Repeat with your left foot.

5 Speed up the move so the two taps are very close together. The two taps then become a shuffle.

Tap

VARIATION
FRONT SHUFFLE
This is exactly the same as a shuffle to the side, but done to the front.

VARIATION
SHUFFLE HOP
After the shuffle, hop before you put your foot back on the ground.

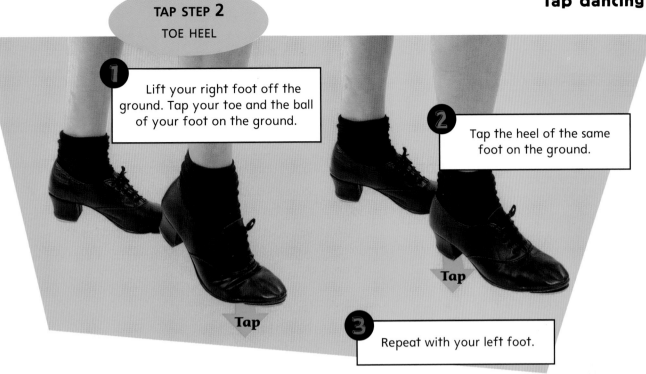

TAP STEP 2

TOE HEEL

1 Lift your right foot off the ground. Tap your toe and the ball of your foot on the ground.

2 Tap the heel of the same foot on the ground.

Tap

Tap

3 Repeat with your left foot.

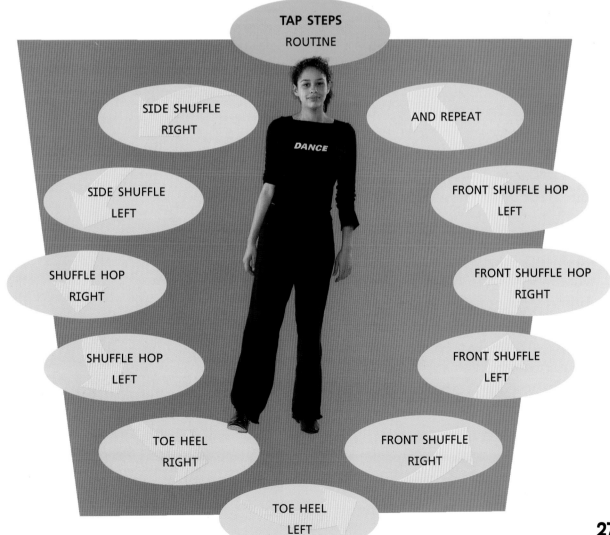

TAP STEPS

ROUTINE

SIDE SHUFFLE RIGHT

AND REPEAT

SIDE SHUFFLE LEFT

FRONT SHUFFLE HOP LEFT

SHUFFLE HOP RIGHT

FRONT SHUFFLE HOP RIGHT

SHUFFLE HOP LEFT

FRONT SHUFFLE LEFT

TOE HEEL RIGHT

FRONT SHUFFLE RIGHT

TOE HEEL LEFT

Street jazz to modern dance

From its early beginnings on the streets of New York, street jazz has evolved in lots of different directions.

The Broadway stage

The early street jazz dances began to appear in cabaret acts in places such as the Cotton Club in Harlem and in dance shows such as *Shuffle Along*.

These small-scale shows were so popular that the big theaters on Broadway soon got in on the act. Stage shows featuring the charleston and the black bottom became all the rage in the 1920s.

From stage to screen

Early movies were all silent, because it was not known how to add a soundtrack to film. In 1927, a movie called *The Jazz Singer* was the first movie to have sound. Because singing and dancing could now be shown to full effect, many Broadway shows were made into movies. A dance choreographer called Busby Berkeley became famous for using dance in movies in a really creative way, with the dancers making stunning visual effects based on complicated patterns.

Dancers in the Busby Berkeley movie *Golddiggers of 1937*.

Dancing in the Depression

In the 1930s, the U.S. was in the middle of the Great Depression, a time when the country's economy was doing very badly. Many people were unemployed and had little money.

One way of trying to earn money was to enter a street-jazz dance marathon in the hope of winning a prize. At these dance marathons, couples danced for as long as they could before collapsing with exhaustion. The prize money was not much, but the determined contestants endured great physical hardship trying to win.

Hollywood musicals

In the 1940s, tap dancing (which had been an important part of street-jazz dance in Harlem) made it into the movies. Stars, such as Gene Kelly, and Fred Astaire and Ginger Rogers, performed elegant, highly choreographed tap routines.

The rise of the choreographer

Dance shows on stage, and musical movies, were hugely popular in the 1940s and 1950s. The choreographers of these shows and movies became almost more important than the directors and producers. Two choreographers, Jerome Robbins and Bob Fosse, were very influential, with shows and movies such as *West Side Story* and *Chicago*.

The modern musical

The tradition of musicals has thrived over the years. Broadway and the West End, in London, have a tradition of staging highly imaginative shows with modern dance routines. In recent years, *Cats*, *The Lion King*, and *Starlight Express* have all attracted huge audiences.

Tap dancing

Tap dancing has survived a dip in popularity and is now once again part of the scene in musical theater and movies. In the U.S., shows such as *Bring in Da Noise*, *Bring in Da Funk* have thrilled modern Broadway audiences. In the UK, *Riverdance* and *Stomp* have firmly established the popularity of modern tap dancing.

Modern dance

Another strand of street-jazz dance developed into a type of modern dance that rivals ballet as an art form. Companies such as the Dance Theater of Harlem or the Rambert Dance Company promote new, exciting, and diverse dance and choreography.

Musical theater is as popular today as it has ever been.

Further information

Websites

www.bustamove.com
Animated figures show a variety of hip-hop moves and routines. You can choose from three levels: beginner, intermediate, or advanced.

www.rap.about.com/library/ blbreakdancecoverpage.htm
This is a great site containing just about everything you need in order to learn to breakdance. There are video clips of all the moves and step-by-step instructions of toprock, downrock, popping, locking, and power moves.

www.ehow.com
Type in "Tap steps" and search. Go to "How to Learn Basic Tap Dance Steps" to find instructions for steps called the cramproll and stomp.

The following two websites have details of classes in tap and modern dance throughout the USA.

www.ndca.org
National Dance Council of America.

http://www.usabda.org
USA national dance website.

DVDs

Hip-hop Workout
An easy-to-follow workout and aerobic exercise program.

Stomp Out Loud
Excerpts from the stage show plus some rechoreographed pieces. It includes the famous routine with the brooms.

Note to parents and teachers: Every effort has been made by the Publishers to ensure these websites are suitable for children, they are of the highest educational value, and contain no inappropriate or offensive material. Because of the nature of the Internet, however, it is impossible to guarantee that the contents of these sites will not be altered. We strongly advise that Internet access is supervised by a responsible adult.

Dancing is a fun way to get in shape, but like any form of physical exercise it has an element of risk, particularly if you are unfit, overweight, or suffer from any medical conditions. It is advisable to consult a healthcare professional before beginning any exercise program.

Glossary

Aerobic exercise   Exercise that improves your breathing and circulation.

b-boying   The original name for breakdancing.

Breakdancing   A type of solo dancing that involves rapid acrobatic moves. It is normally performed to rap music.

Capoeira   A type of martial art. Also an Afro-Brazilian dance form that incorporates martial arts movements.

Choreography   The process of arranging the steps of dance routines.

Coordination   The ability to move different parts of the body together at the same time.

Crew   A group of people performing a breakdancing routine together in a dance battle.

Downrock   The second stage of breakdancing, which is performed low on the floor.

Gangsta   A gangster, or gang member.

Graffiti   Messages, names, or paintings spraypainted on walls and buildings in public places.

Hip hop   A popular urban youth culture that includes DJ-ing, rap music, dance, and graffiti art.

Hormone   A substance produced by the body, which affects the way the body functions.

Isolations   A type of exercise involving moving one part of the body without moving the rest.

Kung fu   A Chinese form of combat or self-defense.

Locking   A breakdancing move that "locks" and then releases the joints to give a robotlike movement.

Martial arts   Arts of combat or self-defense, such as karate and judo, which are practiced as a sport.

Moonwalking   A breakdancing move in which the feet appear to glide along the floor.

Percussion   Instruments that are struck to make a sound.

Popping   A breakdancing routine in which the joints are moved in a series of fluid movements.

Power moves   Acrobatic breakdancing moves.

Rap   A style of improvised music with a strong beat.

Toprock   The first stage of breakdancing, done standing upright. It is designed to clear a space on the dancefloor before starting to perform other moves.

Index

This edition first published in 2007 by
Sea-to-Sea Publications
1980 Lookout Drive
North Mankato
Minnesota 56003

Copyright © Sea-to-Sea Publications 2007

Printed in China

Library of Congress Cataloging in Publication Data
Storey, Rita.
  Street jazz/ by Rita Storey.
   p.cm. -- (Get dancing)
  Includes index.
  ISBN-13: 978-1-59771-049-7
  1. Dance--Juvenile literature. Jazz dance--Juvenile literature. I.Title. II. Series.

  GV1596.5.S76 2006
  792.8 – dc22

                2005056767

9 8 7 6 5 4 3 2

Published by arrangement with the Watts Publishing Group Ltd, London

Series editor: Rachel Cooke
Art director: Peter Scoulding
Series designed and created for Franklin Watts by STOREYBOOKS Ltd.
Designer: Rita Storey
Editor: Fiona Corbridge
Photography: Tudor Photography, Banbury
Dance consultant: Lucie-Grace Welsman

Picture credits
Corbis/Patrik Giardino p. 9; Corbis/Jeremy Bembaron p. 23;
Corbis/Bettmann p. 28.

Cover images: Tudor Photography, Banbury.

Every attempt has been made to clear copyright. Should there be any
inadvertent omissions, please apply to the publisher for rectification.

All photos posed by models.

Thanks to James Boyce, Kimesha Campbell,

Amba Mann, Grace Penman, Charlie Storey, Hannah Storey and

Michael Williams.

With many thanks to Goody Two Shoes, Rugby, UK, who supplied all the
costumes.